BLACK LIVES MATTER

Martin Luther King Inspirational Quotes

Alexander Lamek

ISBN: 9798556417861

Our lives begin to end
the day we become silent
about things that matter.

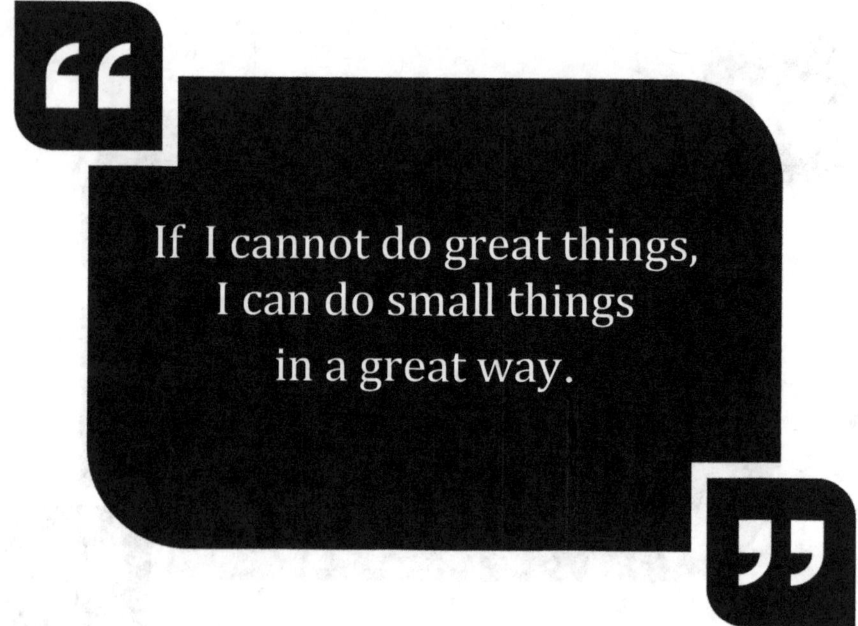
If I cannot do great things,
I can do small things
in a great way.

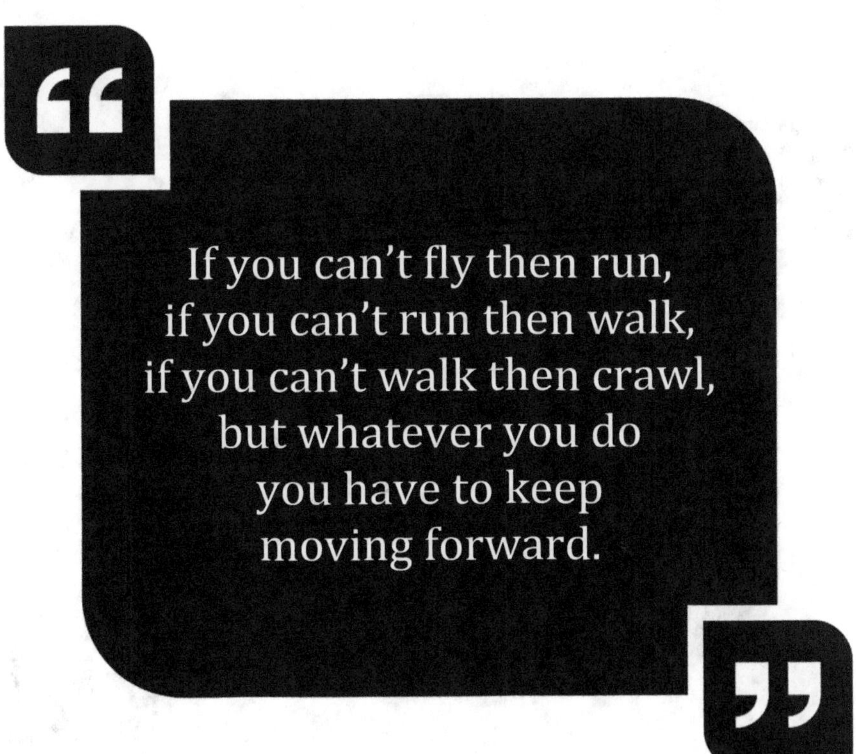
If you can't fly then run,
if you can't run then walk,
if you can't walk then crawl,
but whatever you do
you have to keep
moving forward.

Lightning makes no sound
until it strikes.

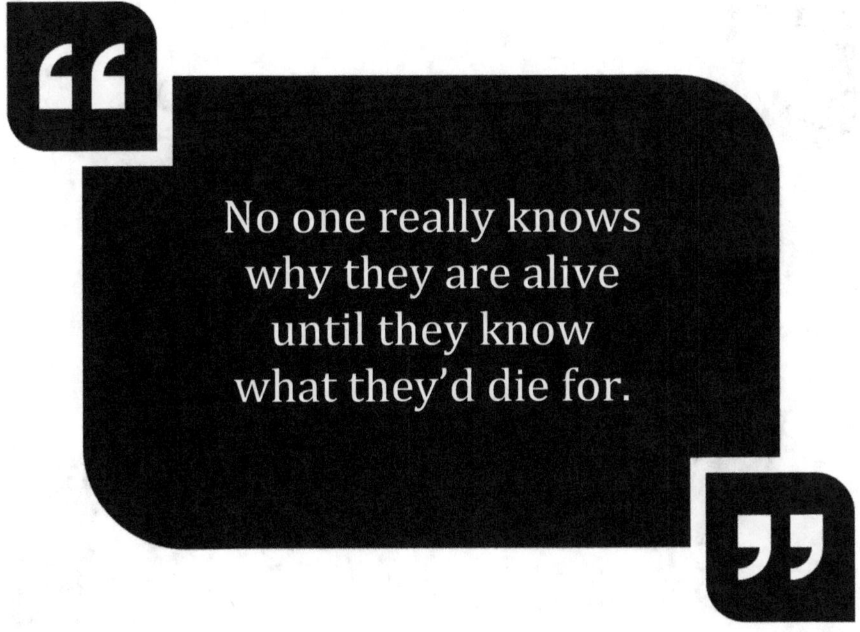
No one really knows
why they are alive
until they know
what they'd die for.

Only in the darkness
can you see the stars.

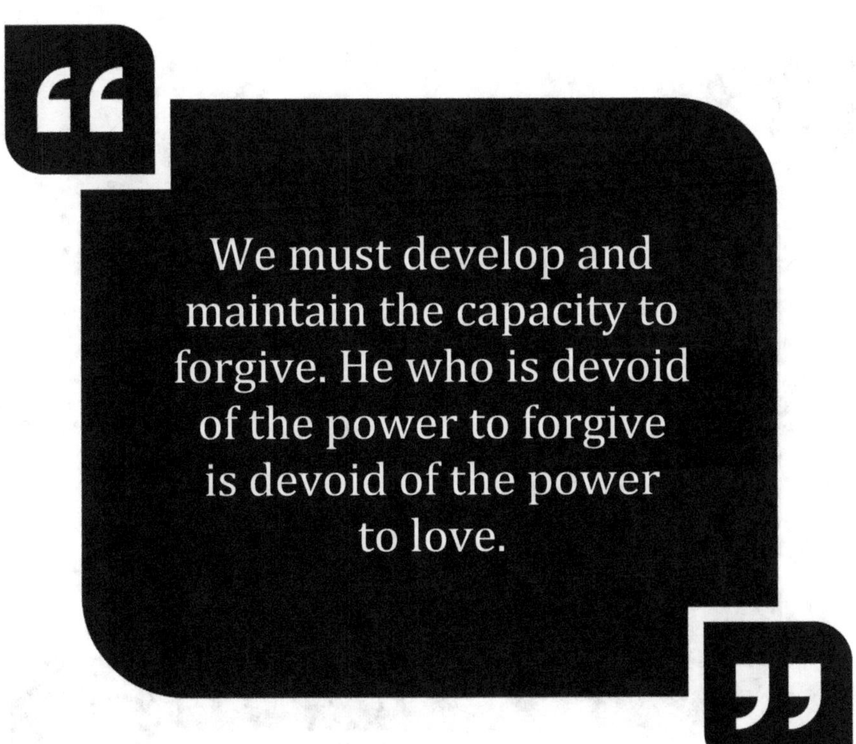
We must develop and
maintain the capacity to
forgive. He who is devoid
of the power to forgive
is devoid of the power
to love.

No, no, we are not satisfied,
and we will not be satisfied
until justice rolls down
like waters and righteousness
like a mighty stream.

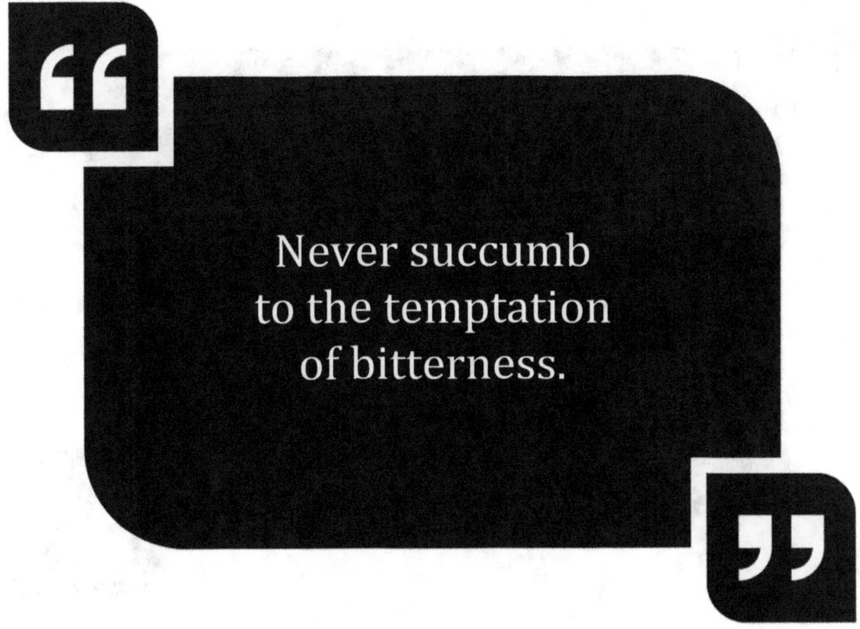
Never succumb
to the temptation
of bitterness.

We are not makers of history.
We are made by history.

Nonviolence is absolute
commitment to the way of love.
Love is not emotional bash;
it is not empty sentimentalism.
It is the active outpouring
of one's whole being into
the being of another.

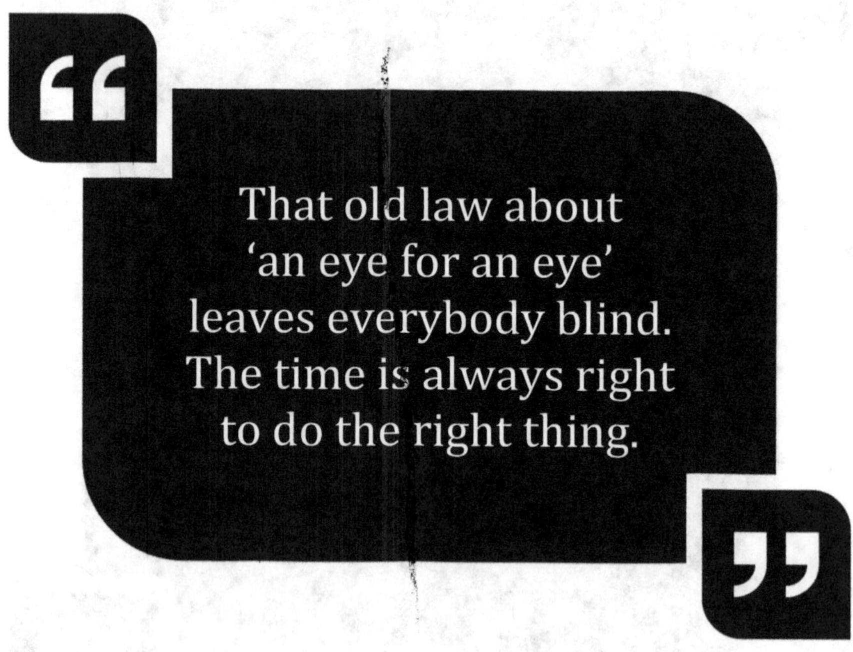
That old law about
'an eye for an eye'
leaves everybody blind.
The time is always right
to do the right thing.

Now there is a final reason I think that Jesus says, 'Love your enemies.' It is this: that love has within it a redemptive power. And there is a power there that eventually transforms individuals. Just keep being friendly to that person. Just keep loving them, and they can't stand it too long.

We cannot walk alone.

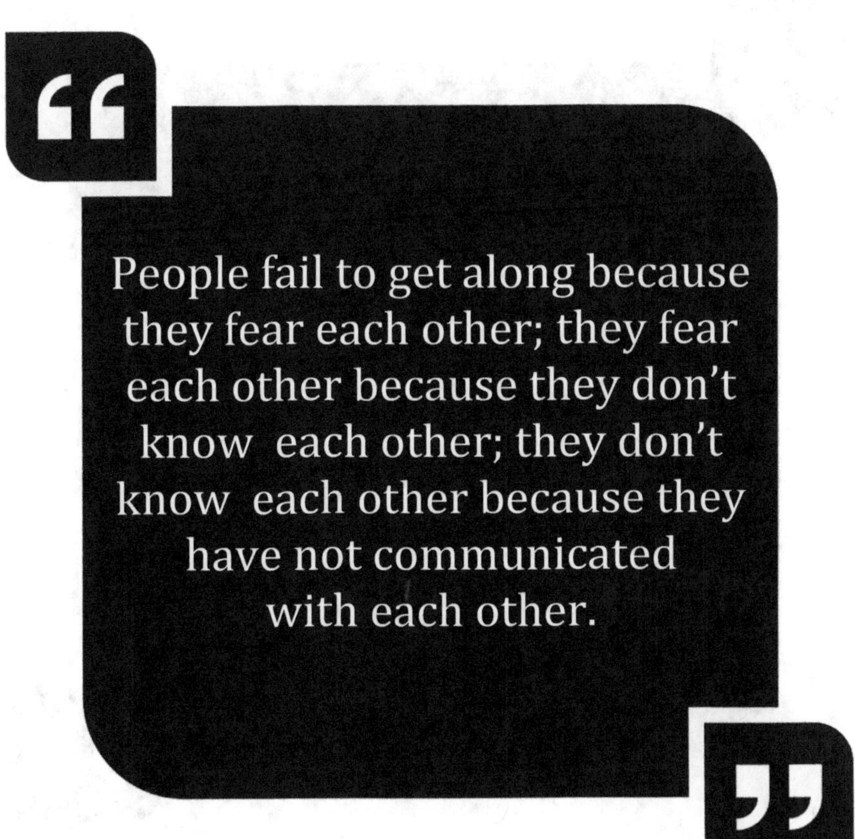
People fail to get along because they fear each other; they fear each other because they don't know each other; they don't know each other because they have not communicated with each other.

We must forever conduct our struggle on the high plane of dignity and discipline. We must not allow our creative protest to degenerate into physical violence. Again and again, we must rise to the majestic heights of meeting physical force with soul force.

A lie cannot live.

A man who won't die for
something is not fit to live.

Injustice anywhere is a threat
to justice everywhere.

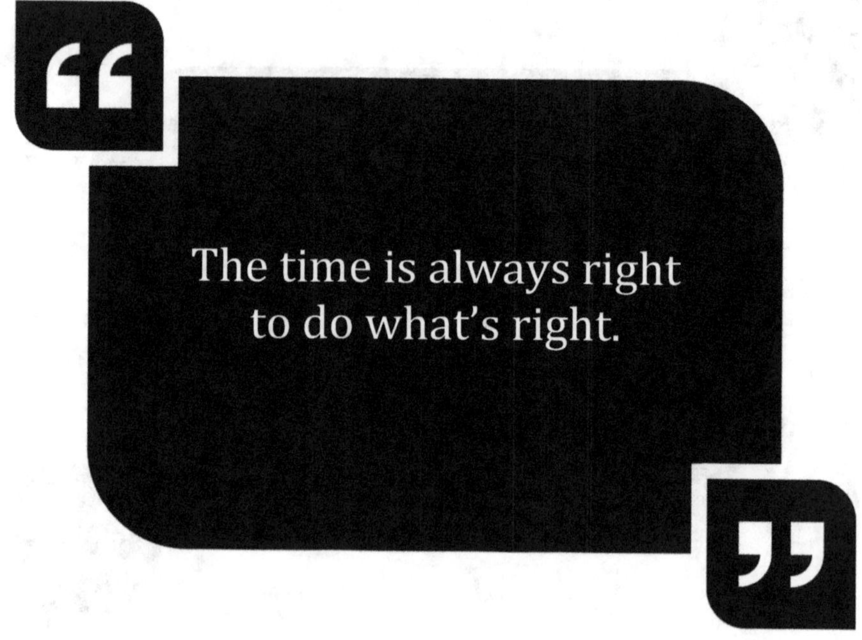
The time is always right
to do what's right.

21

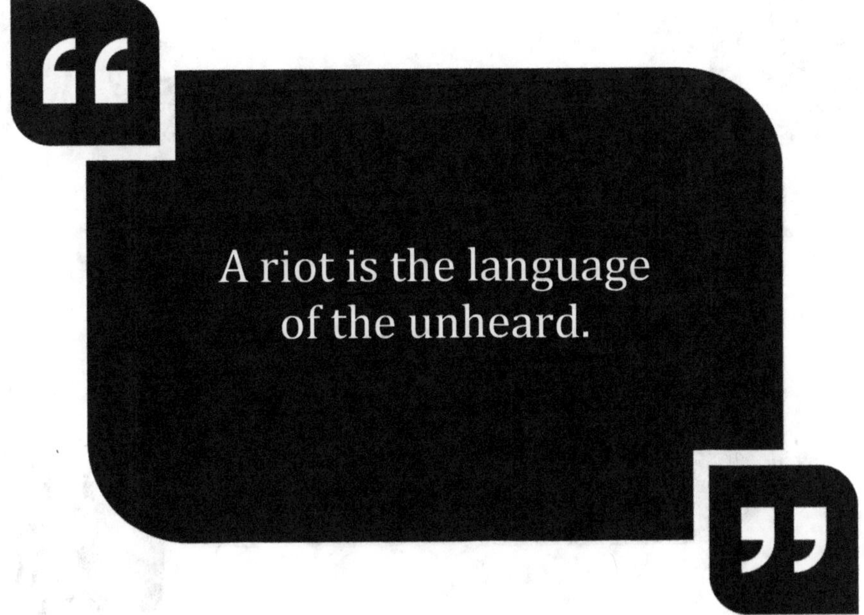

Nonviolence is a powerful and
just weapon. which cuts
without wounding and ennobles
the man who wields it.
It is a sword that heals.

If any earthly institution or custom conflicts with God's will, it is your Christian duty to oppose it. You must never allow the transitory, evanescent demands of man-made institutions to take precedence over the eternal demands of the Almighty God.

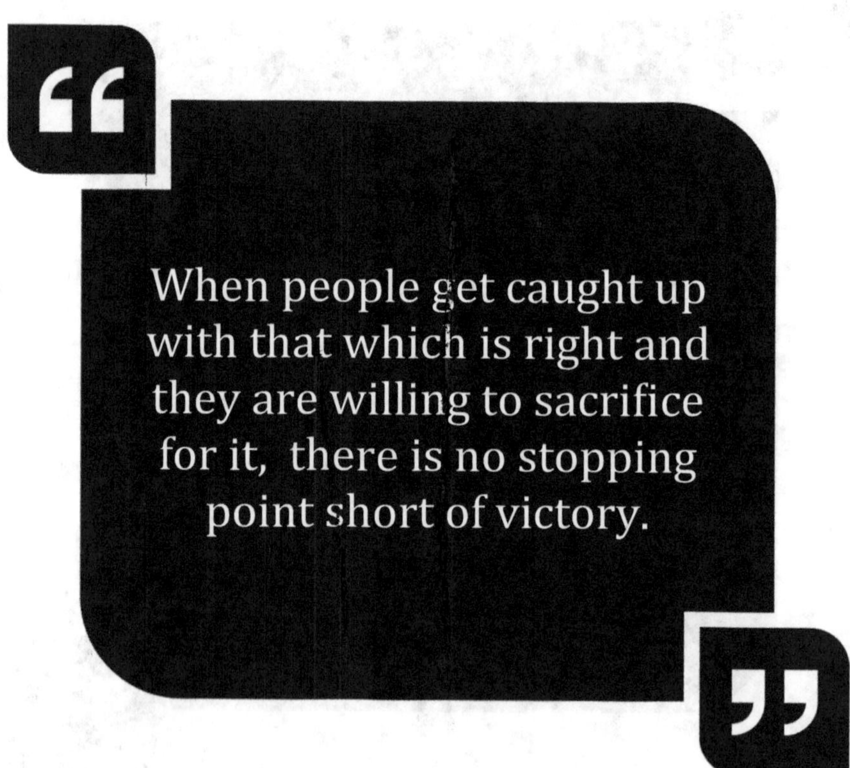
When people get caught up
with that which is right and
they are willing to sacrifice
for it, there is no stopping
point short of victory.

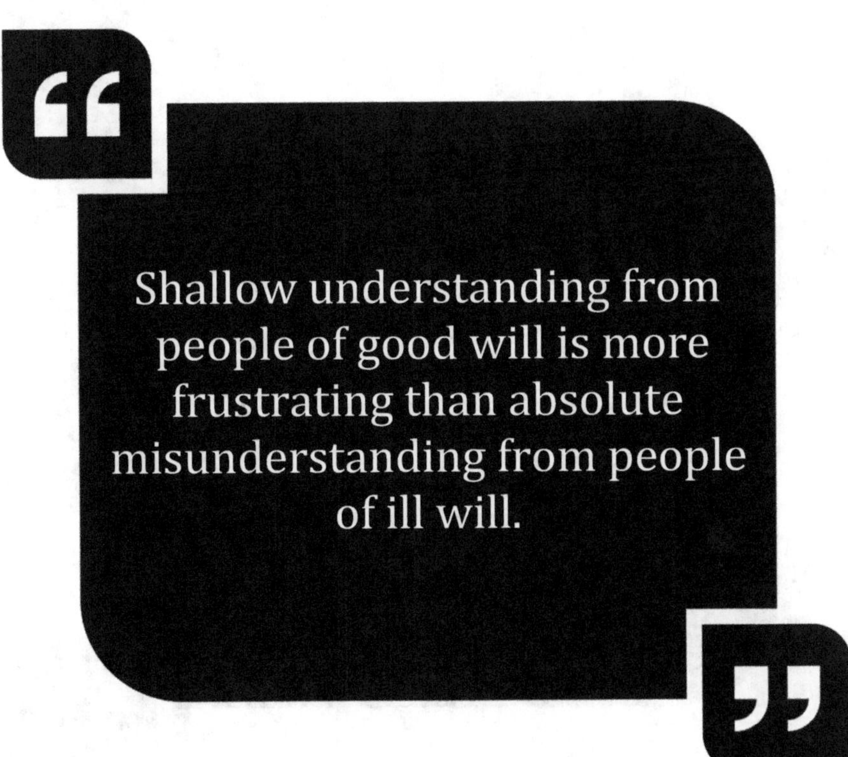
Shallow understanding from people of good will is more frustrating than absolute misunderstanding from people of ill will.

Everything that we see
is a shadow cast by that
which we do not see.

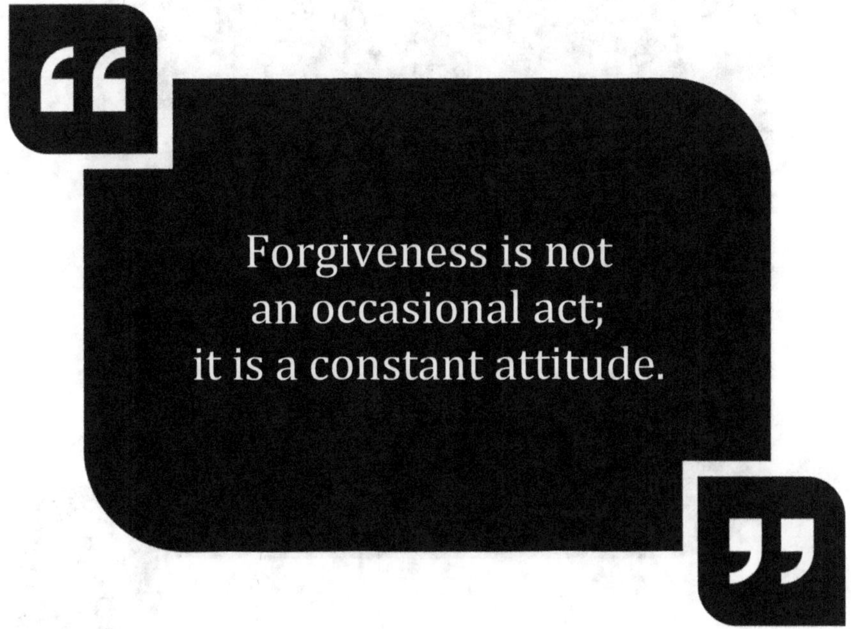
Forgiveness is not
an occasional act;
it is a constant attitude.

I came to the conclusion that there is an existential moment in your life when you must decide to speak for yourself; nobody else can speak for you.

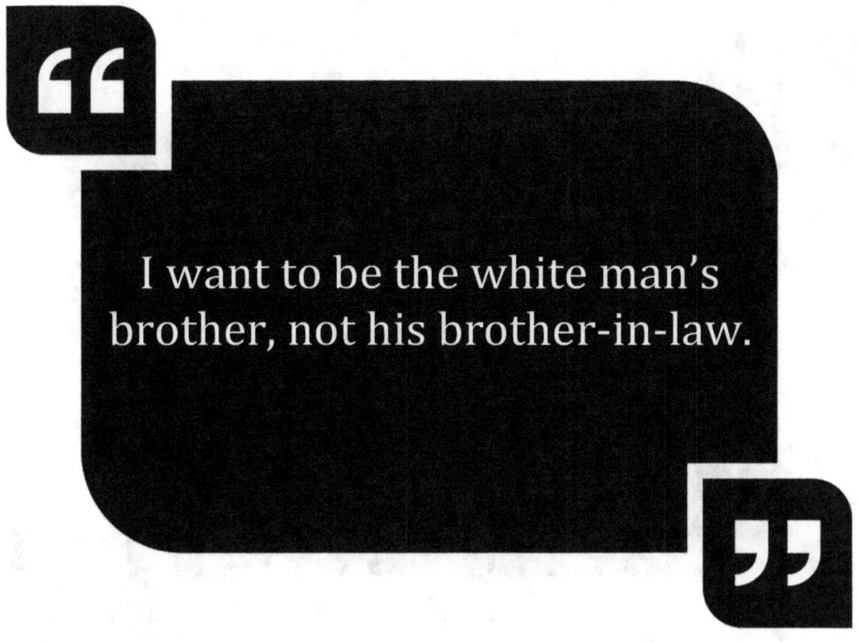
I want to be the white man's brother, not his brother-in-law.

He who is devoid of the power
to forgive is devoid of
the power to love.

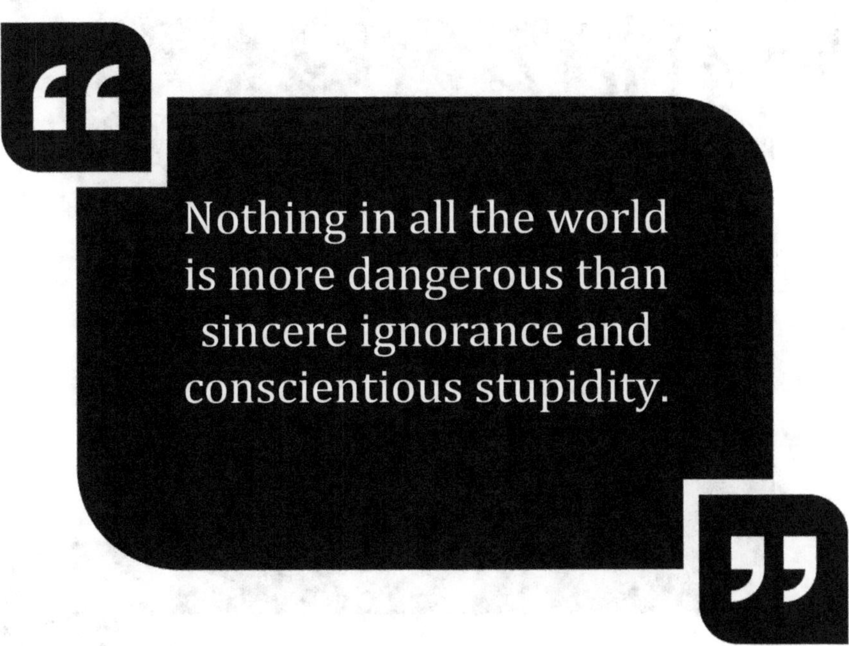
Nothing in all the world
is more dangerous than
sincere ignorance and
conscientious stupidity.

I have a dream that my
four little children will one day
live in a nation where they will
not be judged by the color
of their skin, but by the content
of their character.

I submit that an individual who breaks a law that conscience tells him is unjust, and who willingly accepts the penalty of imprisonment in order to arouse the conscience of the community over its injustice, is in reality expressing the highest respect for law.

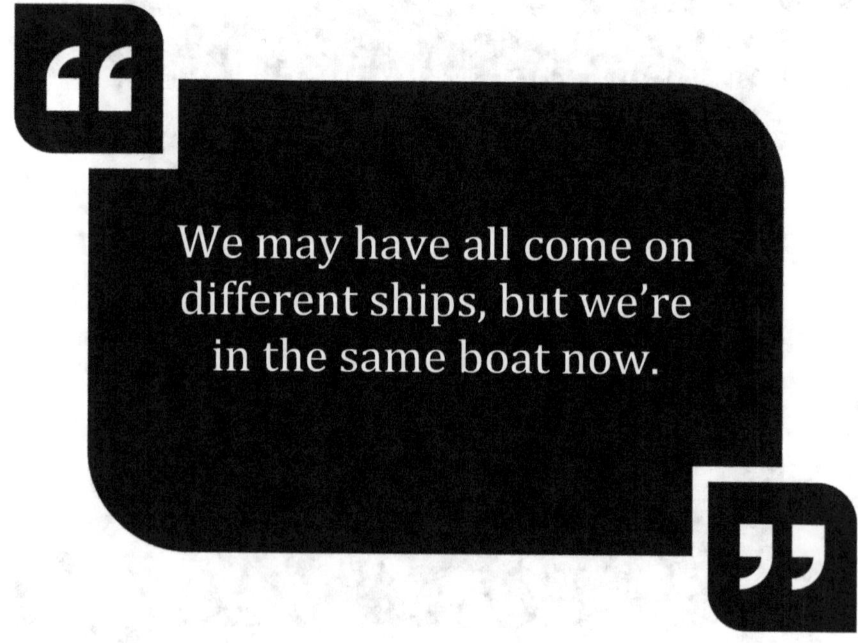
We may have all come on
different ships, but we're
in the same boat now.

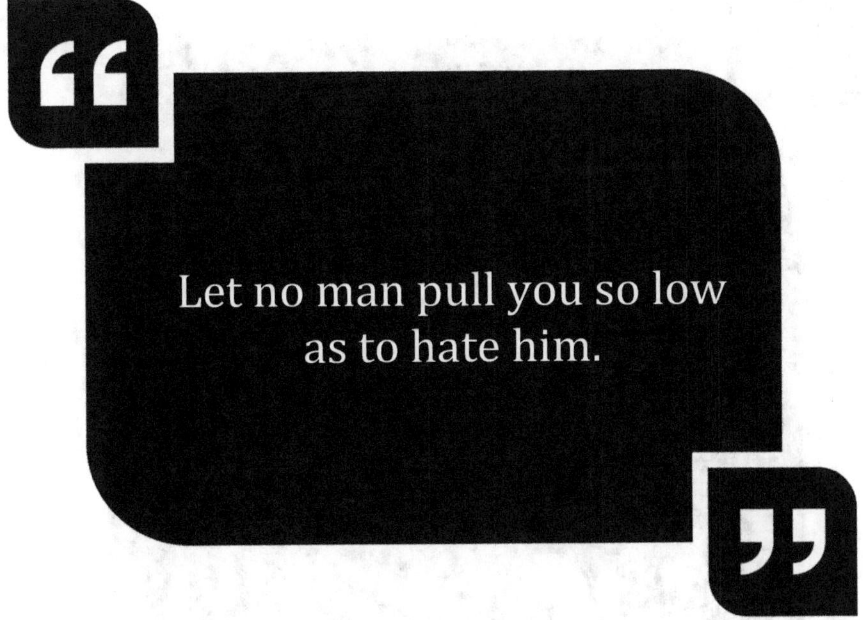
Let no man pull you so low
as to hate him.

Returning hate for hate multiplies hate, adding deeper darkness to a night already devoid of stars.
Darkness cannot drive out darkness; only light can do that.
Hate cannot drive out hate; only love can do that.

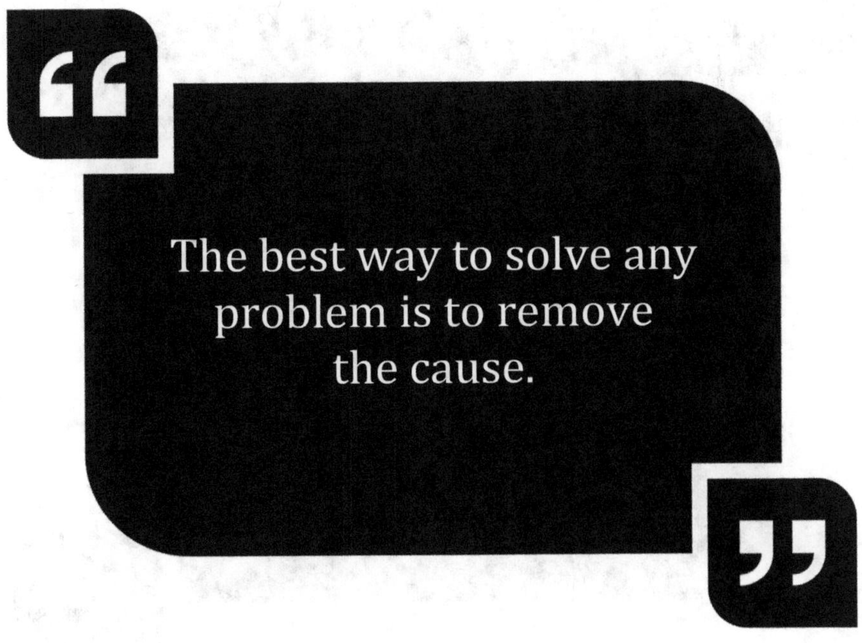

The best way to solve any
problem is to remove
the cause.

Nonviolence means avoiding not only external physical violence but also internal violence of spirit. You not only refuse to shoot a man, but you refuse to hate him.

Man must evolve for all human conflict a method which rejects revenge, aggression and retaliation. The foundation of such a method is love.

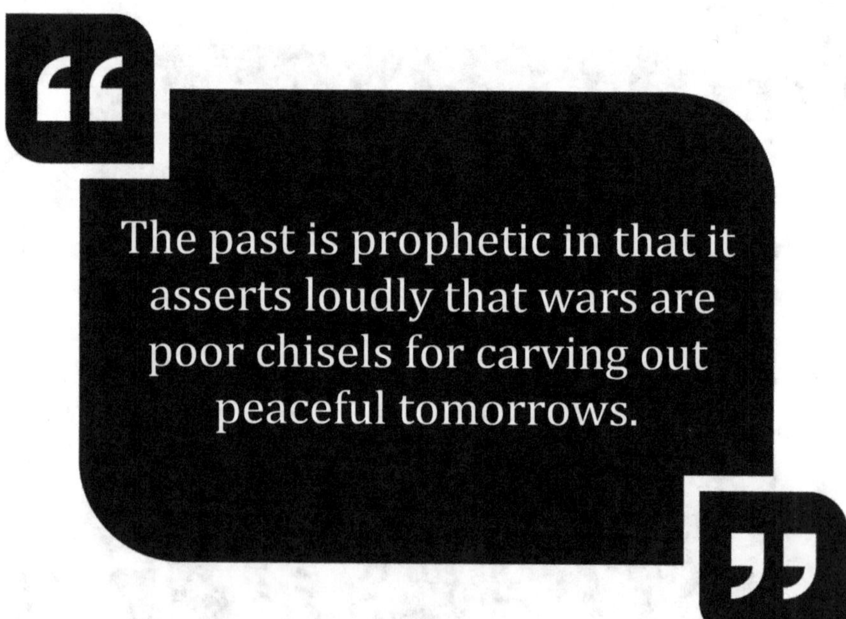
The past is prophetic in that it asserts loudly that wars are poor chisels for carving out peaceful tomorrows.

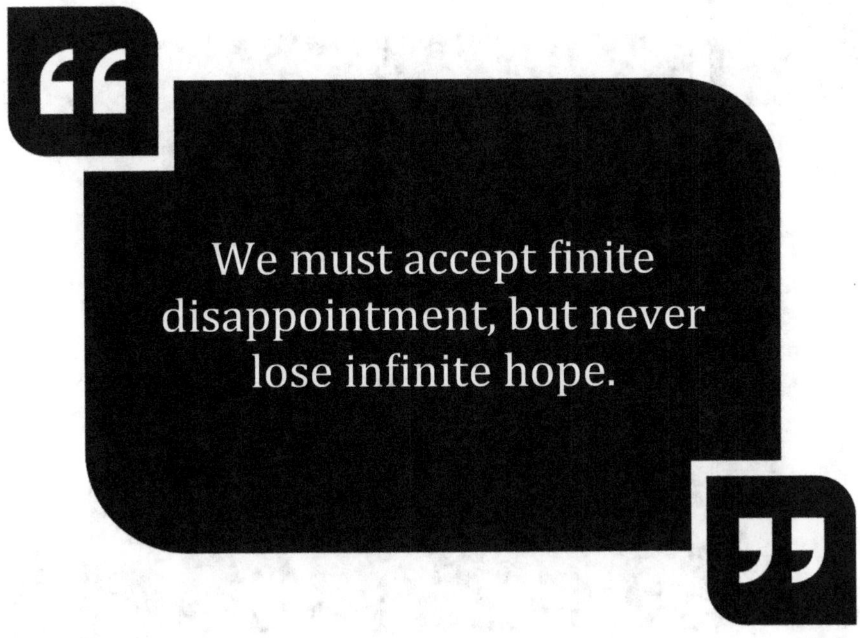

We must accept finite disappointment, but never lose infinite hope.

If you have weapons, take them home; if you do not have them, please do not seek to get them. We cannot solve this problem through retaliatory violence.

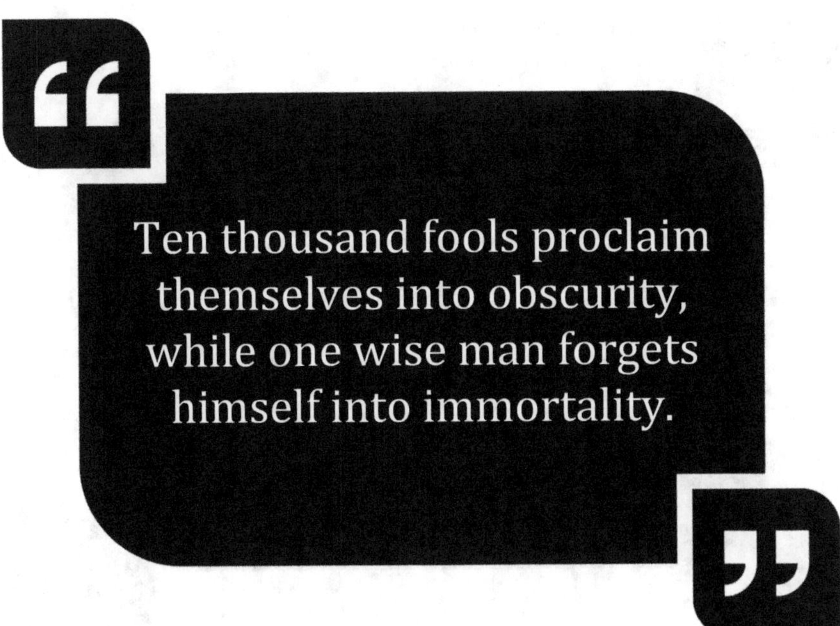
Ten thousand fools proclaim themselves into obscurity, while one wise man forgets himself into immortality.

Take the first step in faith.
You don't have to see
the whole staircase,
just take the first step.

You will change your mind;
You will change your looks;
You will change your smile,
laugh, and ways but no matter
what you change,
you will always be you.

We are prone to judge success by the index of our salaries or the size of our automobiles rather than by the quality of our service and relationship to mankind.

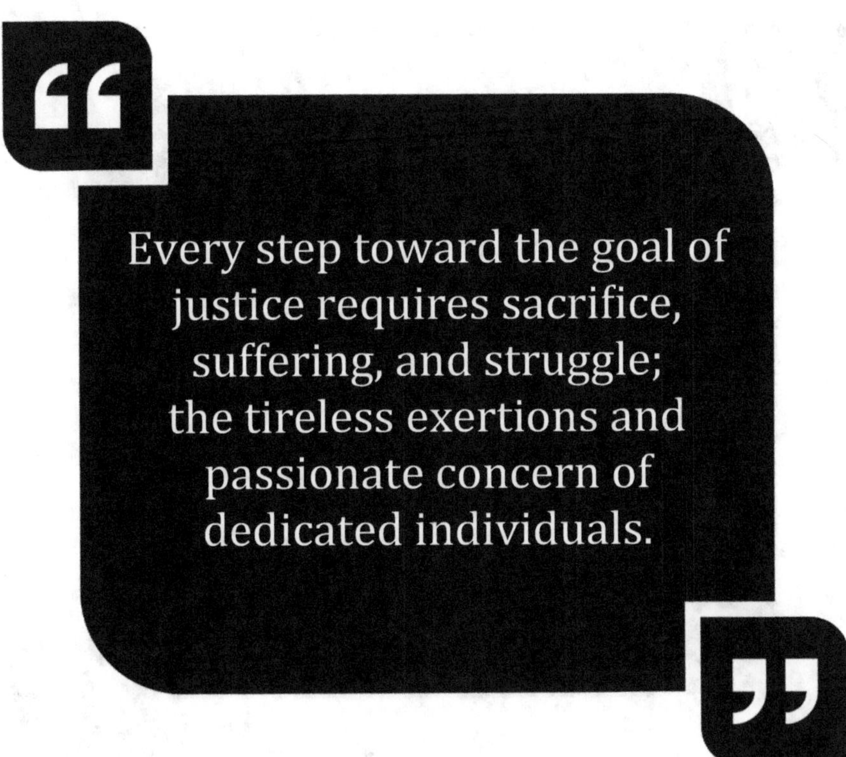
Every step toward the goal of justice requires sacrifice, suffering, and struggle; the tireless exertions and passionate concern of dedicated individuals.

48

The function of education is to teach one to think intensively and to think critically. Intelligence plus character – that is the goal of true education.

The ultimate tragedy is not the oppression and cruelty by the bad people but the silence over that by the good people.

It may be true that the law cannot make a man love me, but it can keep him from lynching me, and I think that's pretty important.

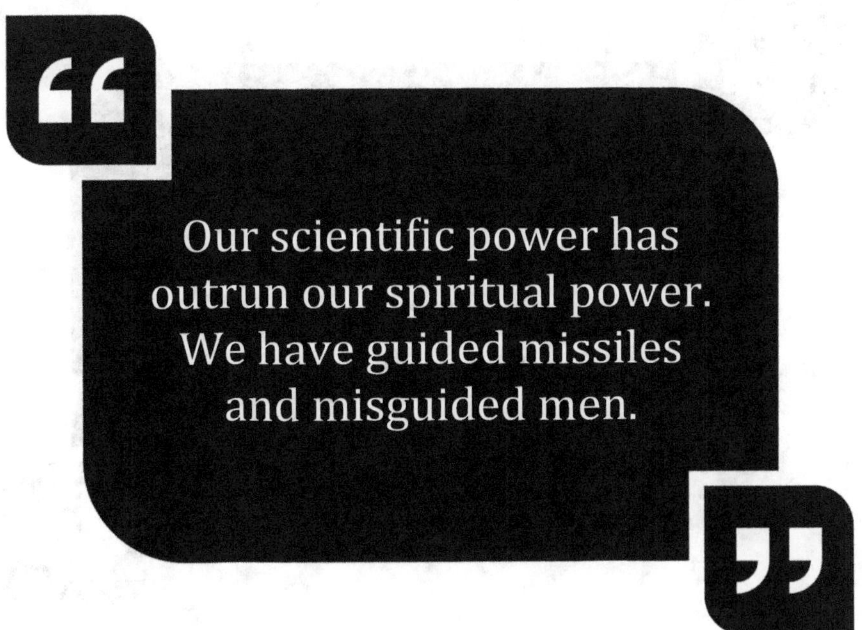
Our scientific power has
outrun our spiritual power.
We have guided missiles
and misguided men.

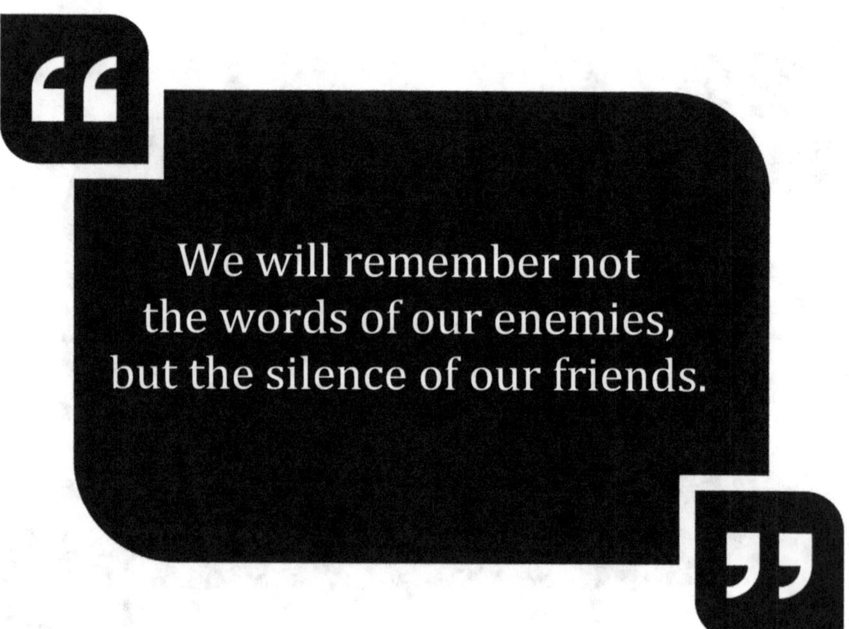
We will remember not
the words of our enemies,
but the silence of our friends.

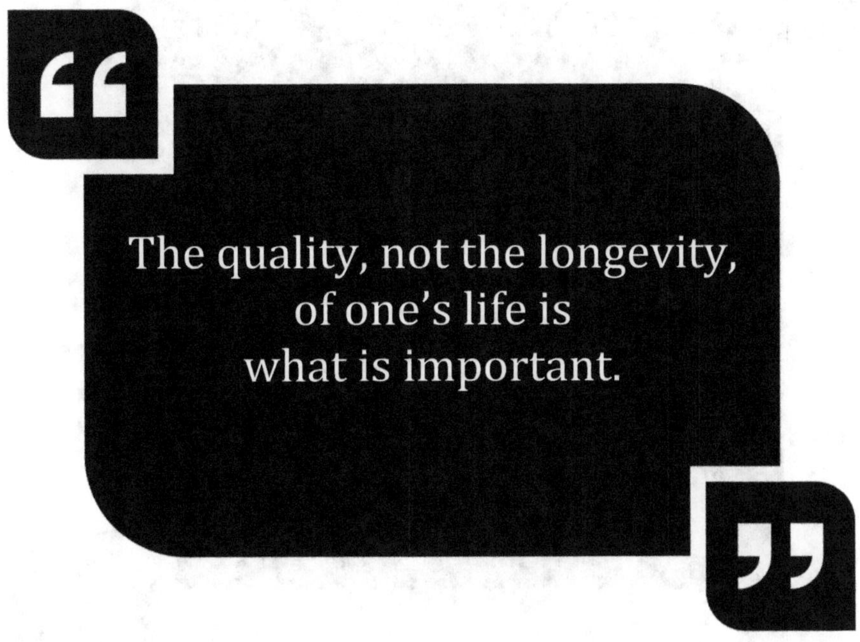
The quality, not the longevity,
of one's life is
what is important.

Those who are not looking for happiness are the most likely to find it, because those who are searching forget that the surest way to be happy is to seek happiness for others.

People fail to get along because they fear each other; they fear each other because they don't know each other; they don't know each other because they have not communicated with each other.

I believe that unarmed truth
and unconditional love will
have the final word in reality.
This is why right, temporarily
defeated, is stronger than
evil triumphant.

Man is man because he is free to operate within the framework of his destiny. He is free to deliberate, to make decisions, and to choose between alternatives. He is distinguished from animals by his freedom to do evil or to do good and to walk the high road of beauty or tread the low road of ugly degeneracy.

We who in engage in nonviolent
direct action are not
the creators of tension.
We merely bring to the surface
the hidden tension that
is already alive.

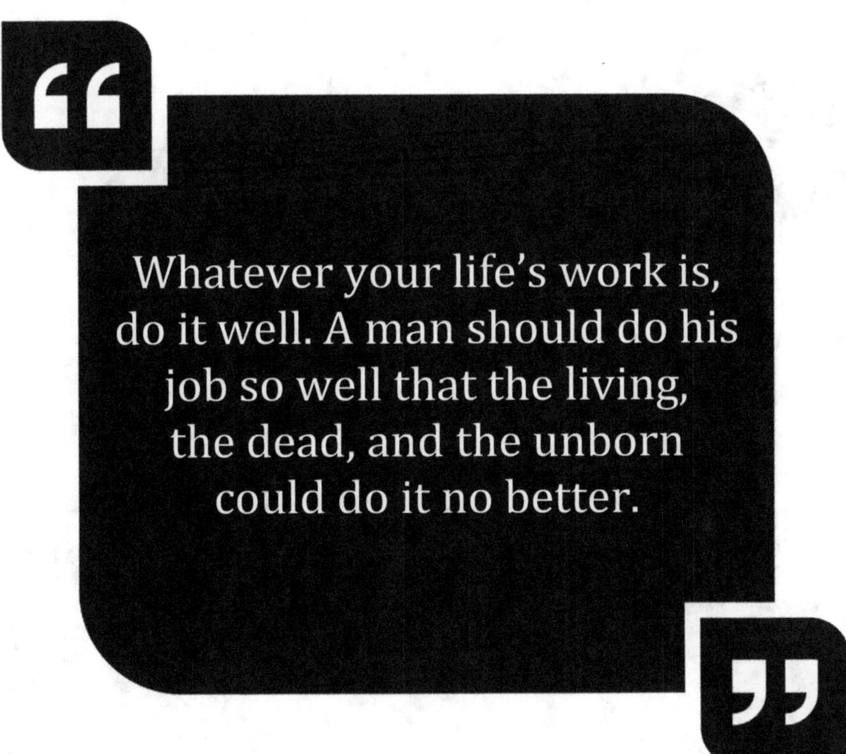
Whatever your life's work is,
do it well. A man should do his
job so well that the living,
the dead, and the unborn
could do it no better.

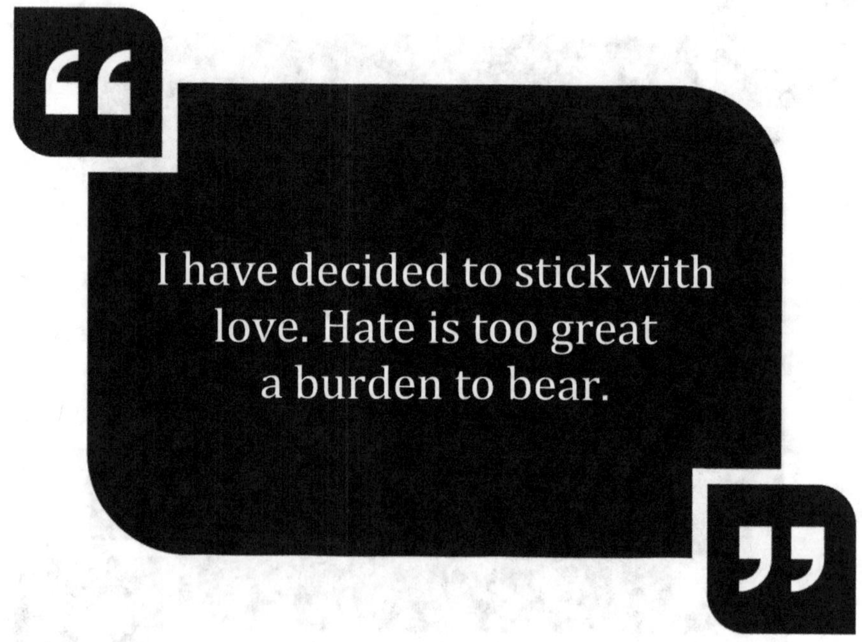
I have decided to stick with
love. Hate is too great
a burden to bear.

If the cruelties of slavery could not stop us, the opposition we now face will surely fail. Because the goal of America is freedom, abused and scorned tho' we may be, our destiny is tied up with America's destiny.

62

Everybody can be great because anybody can serve. You don't have to have a college degree to serve. You don't have to make your subject and verb agree to serve. You only need a heart full of grace.
A soul generated by love.

History will have to record that
the greatest tragedy of this
period of social transition was
not the strident clamor of
the bad people, but the appalling
silence of the good people.

Every man must decide whether
he will walk in the light of
creative altruism or
in the darkness of
destructive selfishness.

The ultimate measure of a man is not where he stands in moments of comfort and convenience, but where he stands at times of challenge and controversy.

World peace through nonviolent means is neither absurd nor unattainable. All other methods have failed. Thus we must begin anew.

There comes a time when one must take a position that is neither safe nor politic nor popular, but he must take it because his conscience tells him it is right.

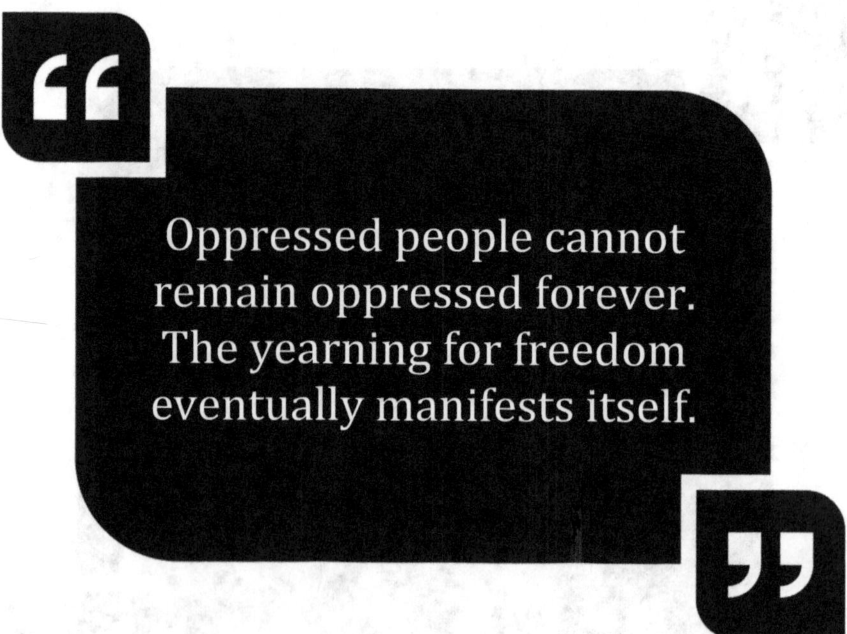
Oppressed people cannot remain oppressed forever. The yearning for freedom eventually manifests itself.

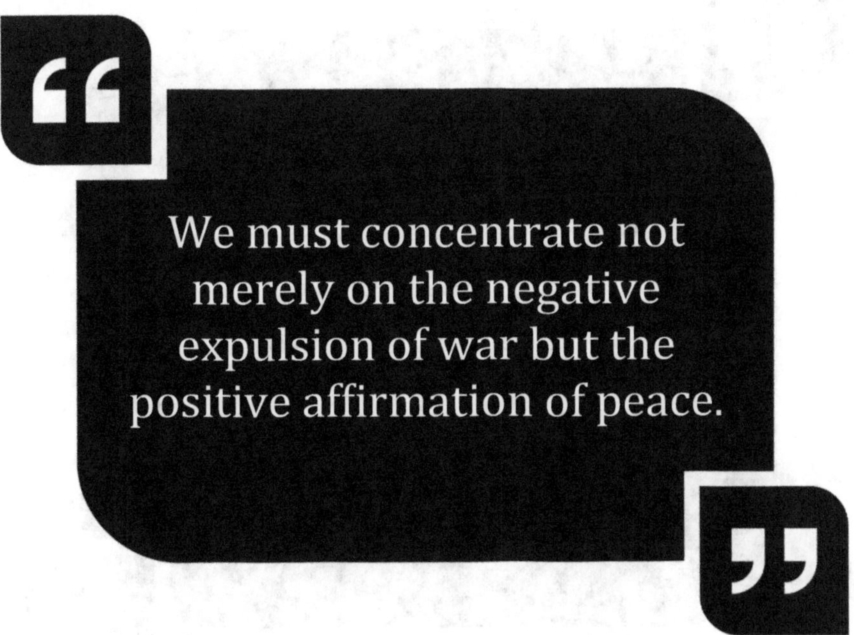
We must concentrate not merely on the negative expulsion of war but the positive affirmation of peace.

The soft-minded man always fears change. He feels security in the status quo, and he has an almost morbid fear of the new. For him, the greatest pain is the pain of a new idea.

Violence as a way of achieving racial justice is both impractical and immoral. I am not unmindful of the fact that violence often brings about momentary results. Nations have frequently won their independence in battle. But in spite of temporary victories, violence never brings permanent peace.

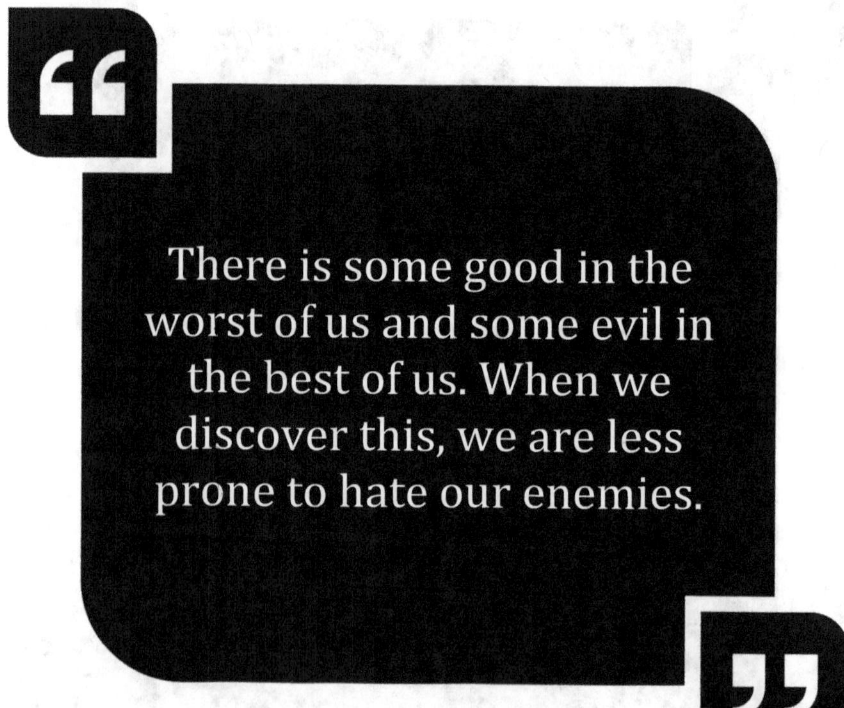
There is some good in the worst of us and some evil in the best of us. When we discover this, we are less prone to hate our enemies.

Courage is an inner resolution
to go forward despite obstacles;
Cowardice is submissive
surrender to circumstances.

74

An individual has not started living until he can rise above the narrow confines of his individualistic concerns to the broader concerns of all humanity.

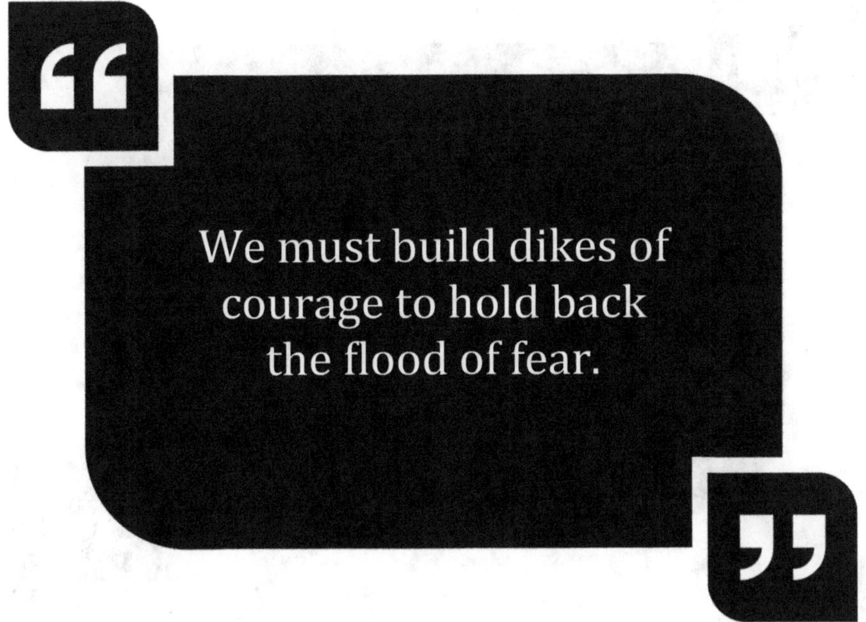
We must build dikes of
courage to hold back
the flood of fear.

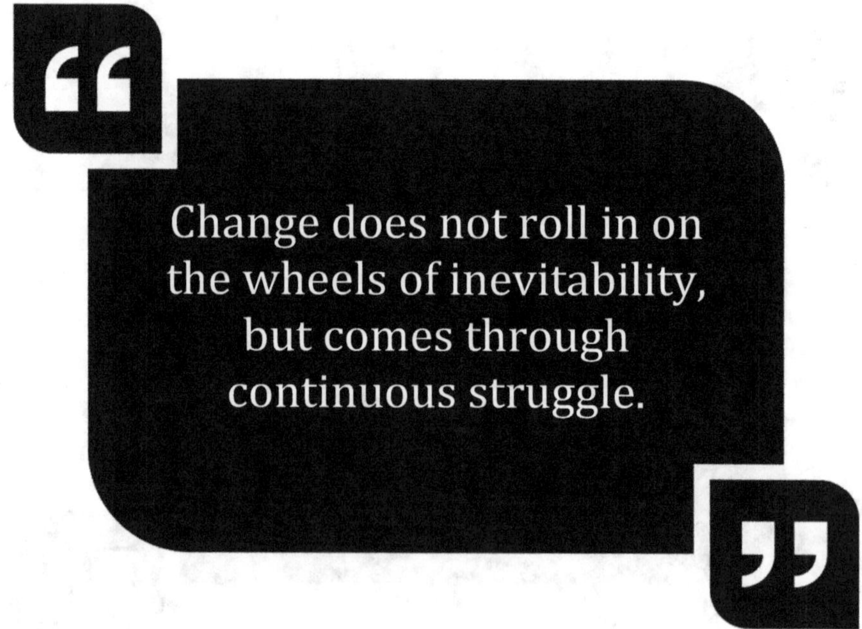
Change does not roll in on
the wheels of inevitability,
but comes through
continuous struggle.

I have a dream that one day little black boys and girls will be holding hands with little white boys and girls.

78

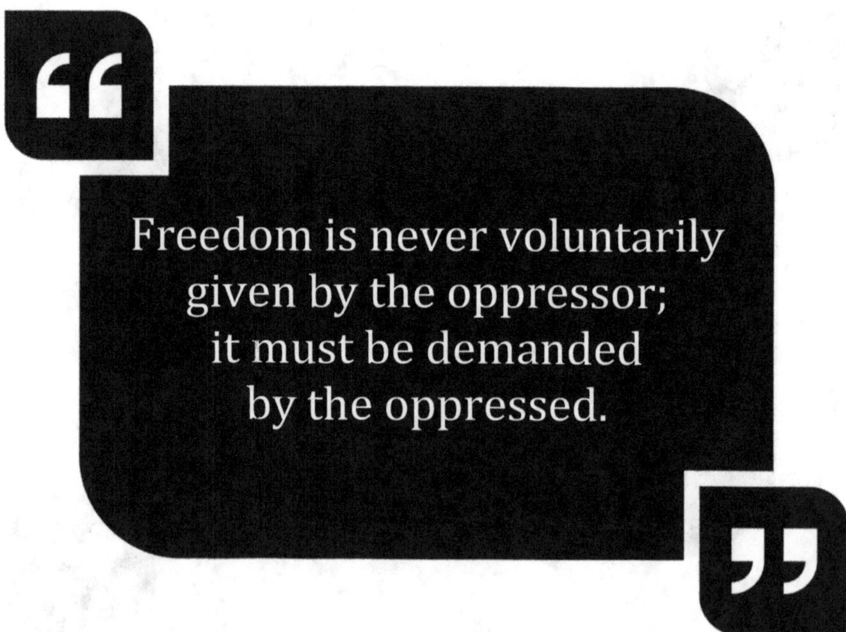
Freedom is never voluntarily
given by the oppressor;
it must be demanded
by the oppressed.

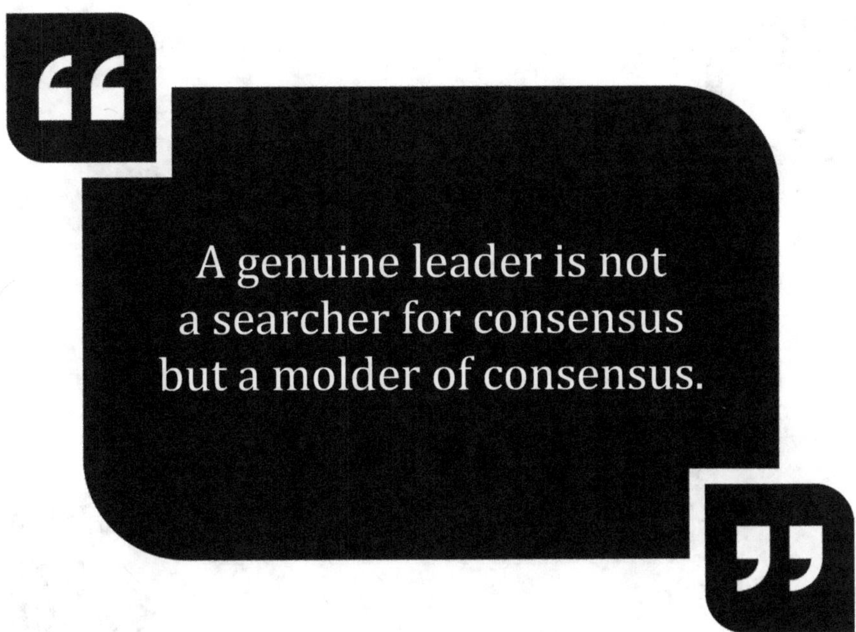
A genuine leader is not
a searcher for consensus
but a molder of consensus.

Almost always, the creative
dedicated minority has made
the world better.

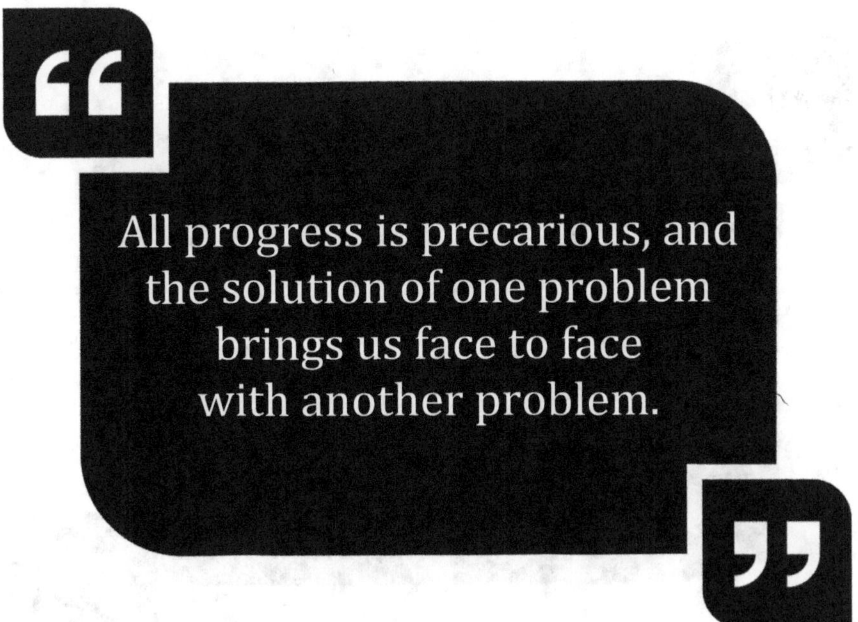
All progress is precarious, and
the solution of one problem
brings us face to face
with another problem.

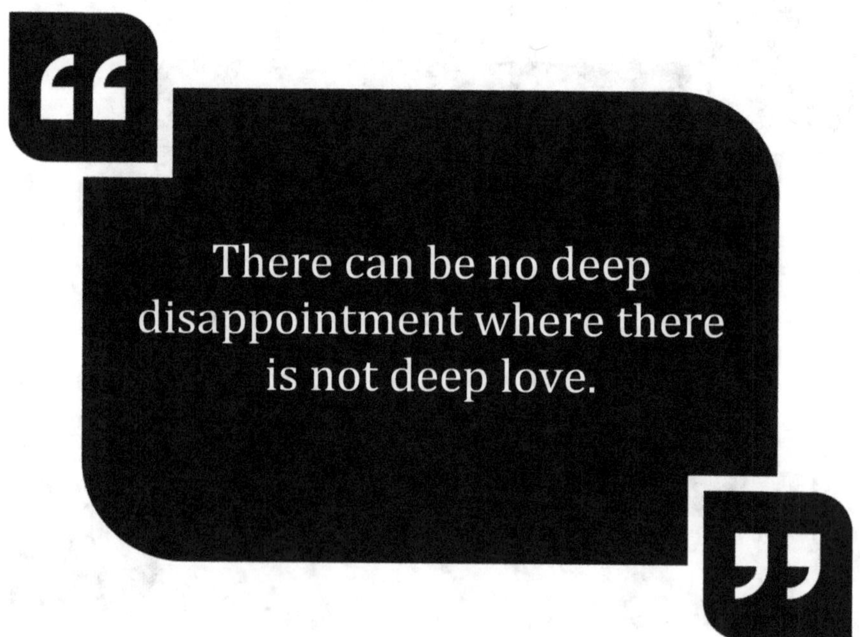
There can be no deep
disappointment where there
is not deep love.

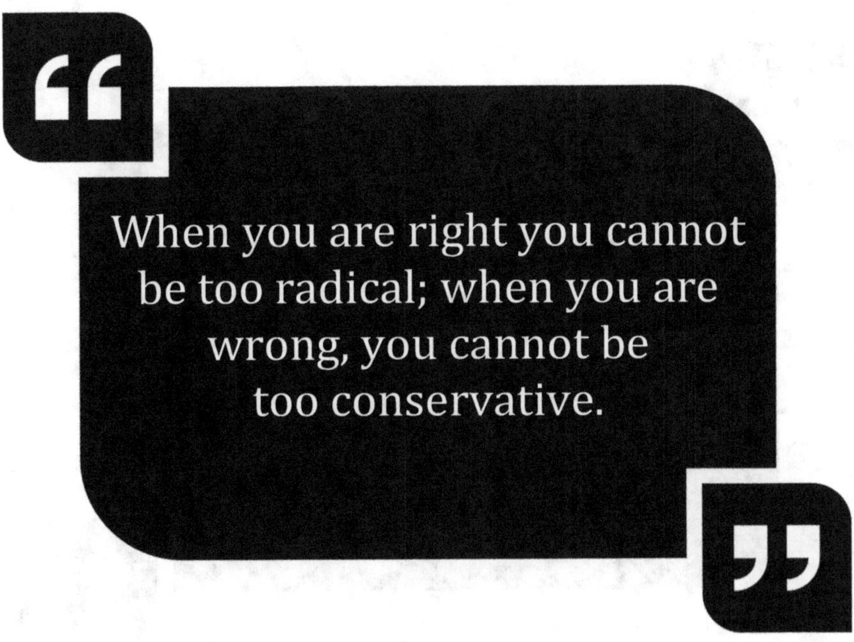
When you are right you cannot
be too radical; when you are
wrong, you cannot be
too conservative.

Never forget that everything
Hitler did in Germany was
"legal".

If physical death is the price
that I must pay to free my
white brothers and sisters
from a permanent death of
the spirit, then nothing
can be more redemptive.

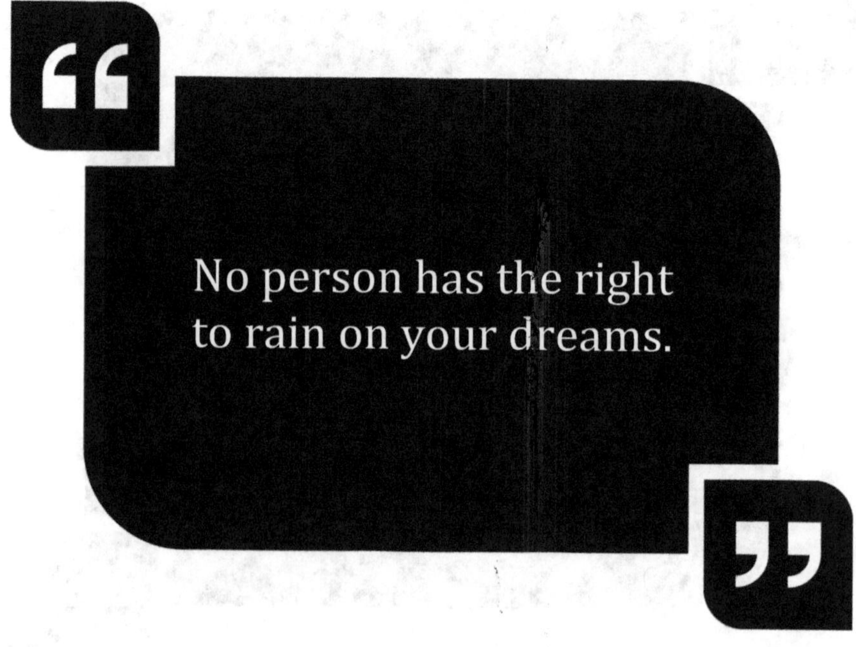
No person has the right
to rain on your dreams.

He who passively accepts evil is as much involved in it as he who helps to perpetrate it. He who accepts evil without protesting against it is really cooperating with it.

We must come to see that
the end we seek is a society
at peace with itself,
a society that can live
with its conscience.

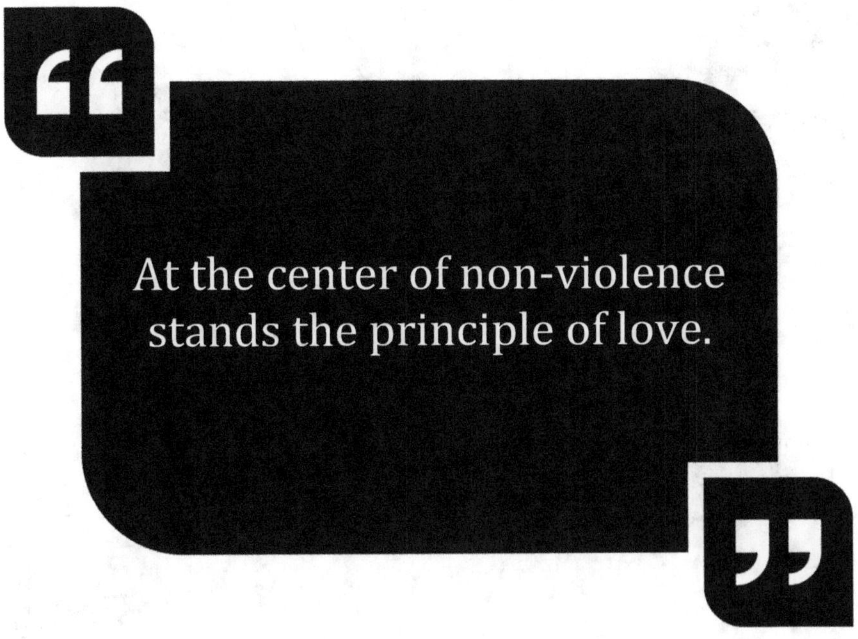
At the center of non-violence
stands the principle of love.

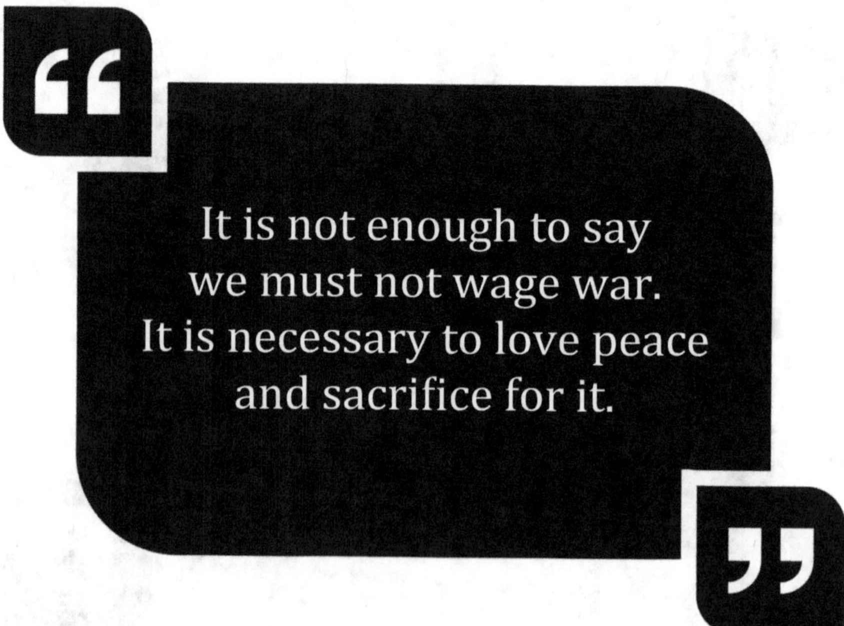
It is not enough to say
we must not wage war.
It is necessary to love peace
and sacrifice for it.

Not everybody can be famous
but everybody can be great
because greatness is
determined by service...
You only need a heart full of
grace and a soul generated
by love.

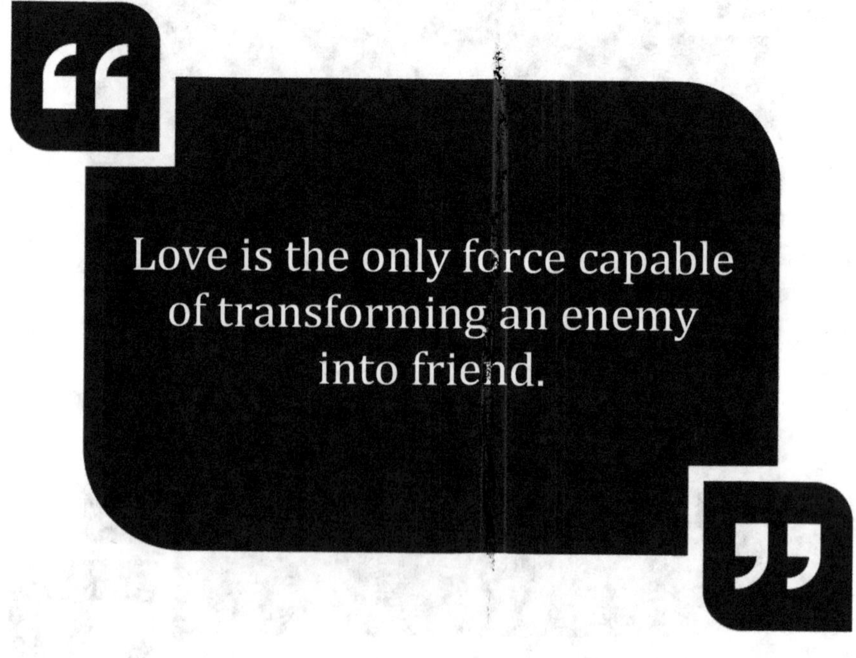
Love is the only force capable
of transforming an enemy
into friend.

Law and order exist for the
purpose of establishing justice
and when they fail in this
purpose they become
the dangerously structured
dams that block the flow of
social progress.

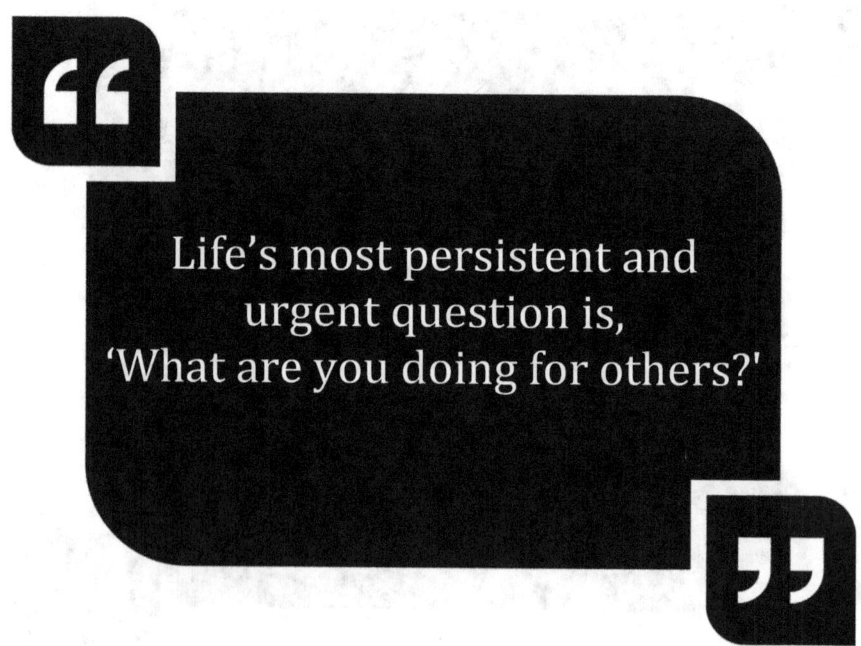
Life's most persistent and
urgent question is,
'What are you doing for others?'

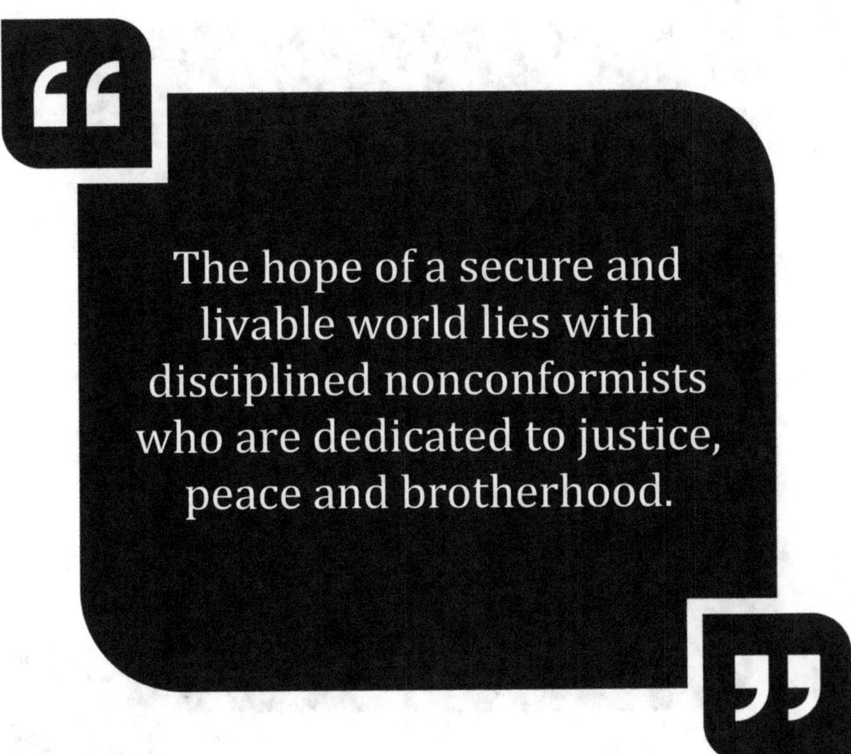
The hope of a secure and livable world lies with disciplined nonconformists who are dedicated to justice, peace and brotherhood.

I refuse to accept the view that mankind is so tragically bound to the starless midnight of racism and war that the bright daybreak of peace and brotherhood can never become a reality... I believe that unarmed truth and unconditional love will have the final word.

Never, never be afraid to do what's right, especially if the well-being of a person or animal is at stake. Society's punishments are small compared to the wounds we inflict on our soul when we look the other way.

I have a dream that one day
every valley shall be exalted,
every hill and mountain shall
be made low, the rough places
will be made straight and
the glory of the Lord shall be
revealed and all flesh shall
see it together.